All Kinds of Books

Susan Canizares
Betsey Chessen

Scholastic Inc.

New York • Toronto • London • Auckland • Sydney

Acknowledgments

Early Childhood Consultant: Ellen Booth Church

Literacy Specialist: Linda Cornwell

Design: Silver Editions

Photo Research: Silver Editions

Endnotes: Sabrina Jones

Endnote Illustrations: Ruth Flanigan

Photographs: Cover: Bill Miles/The Stock Market; p. 1: Michael Newman/Photo Edit; p. 2: David Pollack/The Stock Market; p. 3: Cindy Charles/Photo Edit; pp. 4, 11: Roy Morsch/The Stock Market; p. 5: Myrleen Ferguson/Photo Edit; p. 6: Alan Hicks/Tony Stone Images; p. 7: Tom & DeeAnn McCarthy/The Stock Market; p. 8: G. R. Gainer/The Stock Market; p. 9: Andy Sacks/Tony Stone Images; p. 10: Norbert Schafer/The Stock Market; p. 12: David Woods/The Stock Market.

Library of Congress Cataloging-in-Publication Data
Canizares, Susan, 1960-
All kinds of books/Susan Canizares, Betsey Chessen.
p.cm.--(Learning center emergent readers)
Summary: Examines the many things that reading a book can help you
do, from fixing a bike to finding a friend's phone number to playing pretend.
ISBN 0-439-04607-6 (pbk.: alk. paper)
1. Books and reading--Juvenile literature. [1. Books and reading.]
I. Chessen, Betsey, 1970-. II. Title. III. Series.
Z1003.C17 1998
028--dc21   98-54203
                                                                             CIP AC

2   3   4   5   6   7   8   9   10   08   03   02   01   00   99

There are all kinds of books.

Some can help you make a toy.

Some can help you fix a bike.

Some can help you bake a cake.

Some can help you call a friend.

Some can help you sing a song.

Some can help you play music.

Some can help you learn the alphabet.

Some can help you get the facts.

With books, you can play pretend.

You can cuddle up.

You can even stay up late!

ALL KINDS OF BOOKS

Books are not just for sitting and reading. Books can help you do a lot of things. They can teach you to do things you've never done before. Some of the things you can do with books are very useful and others are just for fun.

Make a toy Activity books are full of projects for children to do, such as making a toy. They use pictures and words to show how to make things step by step. This book has directions and lists of supplies.

Fix a bike A bicycle-repair book can help you keep your bike running fast and safe. It shows how to oil the chain, how to replace worn-out brakes, and how to patch a flat tire. It tells what tools you need to keep a new bike in good shape or to make an old one work like new again.

Bake a cake A cookbook can help you bake a delicious cake! The recipe has a description of the cake, a list of ingredients, instructions, and maybe even some menu ideas for what to serve with it. Recipes are tested by professional cooks before they go into the book.

Call a friend Telephone books are organized by areas, towns, and cities, and are made by the phone company. Everyone who has a telephone in the area is listed in this book. Once a year, new numbers are added, such as those of people who have moved into town, and a new copy is left on everyone's doorstep. To find a number, look for the person's last name in alphabetical order and check the address, too.

Sing a song By following the words and notes in a songbook, you can sing together in time. The first written music was on very big pages so a whole choir could see it and sing together. A songbook can help you learn a new song or remember an old favorite.

Play music Pages of sheet music are often combined into a music book. Music has its own kind of writing, with notes instead of letters. The notes tell this boy where to put his fingers and how long and fast to blow. If he learns to read and play very well, he can play with other musicians in a band or an orchestra.

Learn the alphabet You can use a book to learn the alphabet. Our alphabet started long ago in ancient Rome. Since each letter stands for a sound, it's good for writing many languages. Some languages, such as Chinese, don't use the letters of the alphabet. They are written with characters based on pictures.

Get the facts You can find out almost anything if you look in the right book! An encyclopedia has more information than one person can know, so many writers work on it. Each one writes about what he or she knows best.

Play pretend A storybook can give you ideas for playing with stuffed animals. Some books have pictures and maps of make-believe places where you might pretend to take your animals. History books contain real adventures from long ago you can recreate as you play.

Cuddle up When children read together, one can help the other to learn. Following the pictures and listening is the first step to learning to read by yourself. It can also be twice the fun to share a book with someone close to you.

Stay up late When it is time for bed, it may be too late for you to go out and play, but it's not too late to read a book by flashlight! When you are done with your day but not sleepy yet, it is the perfect time to go to the dream world of books.